Wicked Weather

PATHFINDER EDITION

By Beth Geiger

CONTENTS

Wicked Weather

By Beth Geiger

Tornadoes are wicked storms. Their churning winds often reach 250 miles per hour. Now scientists brave those winds to learn how to predict the deadly storms.

r

At 6:00 p.m. on May 3, 1999, weather forecasters urgently warned that a tornado was twisting toward Oklahoma City. They told people to find a safe place to hide.

On a nearby highway, two trucks ignored the warning. Instead of driving away from the storm, they raced toward it.

Driving Winds

That's right, the two trucks sped toward the storm. Their six occupants were not Hollywood daredevils or thrill seekers. And they knew exactly what they were doing. They were tornado chasers.

Josh Wurman was the group's leader. Wurman is a **meteorologist,** a scientist who studies weather. Unlike most people, Wurman likes bad weather. The nastier, the better. He especially likes tornadoes.

The meteorologists had been waiting all day. That morning, they thought conditions seemed right for tornadoes. They started driving around looking for storms.

Double Trouble. *This photo of two tornadoes was taken by National Geographic photographers making the large–format film* Forces of Nature.

By noon, they were hungry. They stopped at a mini-mart to stock up on candy bars and potato chips. They didn't know it, but their workday was just starting. And it was going to be a blustery day.

By six o'clock, Wurman's crew had already spotted six tornadoes. The biggest was on its way. But why were the scientists chasing tornadoes? And why were they in trucks?

Hit the Road

A few years earlier, Wurman had an idea. He decided to put a weather station in a truck. He even included **Doppler radar.** This equipment tracks storms over hundreds of miles.

Doppler radar is a valuable tool. You've probably seen your local weather forecaster use it on the news. But it has its limits.

The radar equipment works best when it's close to a storm. By putting it on a truck, Wurman hoped to drive as close to a tornado as he could get. By studying twisters up close and learning everything about them, the scientists hope someday to predict the storms.

Twisted. *Circular winds twist a storm cloud. The cloud isn't a tornado, but it could turn into one. Such clouds are called supercells.*

How a Tornado Forms

1. Circular winds develop deep inside a storm cloud.

2. The circular winds move downward. They form a funnel.

3. Downdrafts in the cloud carry hail and rain.

4. Winds near the ground pick up debris. It forms a cloud around the tornado.

5

Alley of Destruction. *LEFT: Most tornadoes in the U.S. form in an area called Tornado Alley. ABOVE: Tornado winds can pick up cars, trees, and almost anything else in the twister's path.*

Twisted Weather

Tornadoes are violently rotating columns of air. They form when a funnel extends from a thundercloud, or a cumulonimbus cloud, to the ground. Small tornadoes can be about 50 feet wide. The largest ones are a mile wide.

Big or small, twisters don't last long—anywhere from 20 seconds to an hour. However, they pack enough force to make your head spin. Tornado winds often top 250 miles per hour.

The roaring winds sound like an out-of-control freight train. They can pick up houses, level neighborhoods, and toss school buses as if they were toys.

Tornado Alley

About 800 tornadoes sweep through the U.S. each year. That's more than in any other country in the world.

Tornadoes can happen at any time and almost anywhere in the United States. They are most common in the spring. And they are more likely in some states than in others.

If you live in Texas, Oklahoma, Colorado, Kansas, Nebraska, South Dakota, Minnesota, or Iowa, you're in twister central! So many tornadoes tear through these states that they're called **Tornado Alley** (see map).

Tornado Alley is twister central because of its geography. What does geography have to do with tornadoes?

Well, the answer is blowing in the wind. Warm air from the Gulf of Mexico washes over Tornado Alley. At the same time, cold air blows down into Tornado Alley from the Rocky Mountains.

Colliding warm and cold air makes the perfect conditions for tornadoes. That's what happened at 6:00 p.m. on May 3, 1999, near Oklahoma City.

Collision Course

By 6:30, the tornado was sweeping across land at 35 miles per hour. It was heading straight for the city. Right behind the tornado raced Wurman's two trucks. Soon the meteorologists were only a minute behind the twister.

Now the winds were whipping around at 100 miles per hour. Cars veered out of control around the trucks. "Pieces of wood and house insulation were raining down out of the clouds," recalls Wurman.

Eventually, the twister broke up. The tornado chasers turned around and drove back to the city. Thousands of homes had been destroyed. Debris was everywhere. No wonder. The team had recorded the highest wind speed ever for a tornado—301 miles per hour!

Saving Lives

May 3, 1999, was one of Dr. Wurman's most action-packed and nerve-racking days ever. But knowing that his work might save lives makes it seem worthwhile. "Plus," says Wurman, "tornadoes are some of the most beautiful and rare things to see."

What are some things you can do to prepare for a tornado or other emergency?

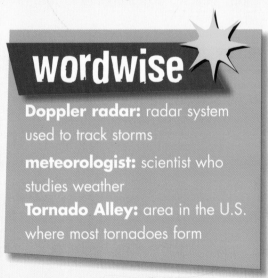

wordwise

Doppler radar: radar system used to track storms

meteorologist: scientist who studies weather

Tornado Alley: area in the U.S. where most tornadoes form

Twisted Feats

Tornadoes are best known for being whirlwinds of destruction. Sometimes twisters perform incredible tricks. At other times, the storms are amazingly gentle. Here are some of their fantastic feats.

November 1915 A twister picked up five horses from their barn. The tornado carried the horses a quarter mile before putting them down unharmed.

November 1915 The same tornado picked up a necktie rack with 10 ties. The rack was found 40 miles away.

June 1939 A tornado plucked the feathers off a chicken.

January 1974 A tornado picked up several empty school buses. The twister hurled the buses more than eight feet in the air.

Tornado Ratings

Tornadoes come in many sizes. So how do we know how big a twister is? Scientists rank the storms on a special scale. This scale rates tornadoes by the speed of their winds and the kinds of damage they do.

The scale has levels ranging from EF0 to EF5. Check out the damage that could happen at each level on the scale below. Then use the scale to rank each tornado described in the eyewitness stories on page 9.

Measuring a Tornado

Level	Wind Speed	Damage
EF0	less than 73 mph (miles per hour)	**Light damage:** Small tree branches broken; light poles shaken; slight damage to mobile homes and roofs of houses.
EF1	73–112 mph	**Moderate damage:** Windows broken; mobile homes pushed off their bases or flipped over; large tree branches broken.
EF2	113–157 mph	**Considerable damage:** Pieces of roof ripped off houses and other buildings; mobile homes destroyed; wooden electrical poles broken.
EF3	158–206 mph	**Severe damage:** Walls of houses, schools, and malls toppled; bark torn off trees; steel electrical poles bent or broken.
EF4	207–260 mph	**Devastating damage:** Houses destroyed; large sections of schools and malls damaged.
EF5	261–318 mph	**Incredible damage:** Schools, malls, and high-rise buildings seriously damaged or destroyed.

How big

Eyewitness Stories: Use the scale to rate each tornado.

Shaking Street Lights

I was riding in the car with my mom and brother when the tornado hit. The winds rattled our car, so mom pulled to the side of the road. A traffic light shook and almost fell off its pole. Trash cans tipped over and blew across the road. But in a few moments, the tornado was gone.

Crushing Homes

Luckily, we weren't home when the tornado touched down. It destroyed many homes in our town. It scattered cars and trucks like toys. Our apartment is now just a heap of rubble. We lost all of our belongings—but we are thankful to be alive. Many people were badly hurt. Some even died during the storm.

Flying Shingles

We were in school when the tornado siren went off. The tornado blew shingles off nearby houses. It also knocked out the power. All the lights went out. Our teacher said that the electrical pole outside the school had snapped in two.

Toppling Trees

We were in the basement when the tornado struck our house. The whole house shook. We heard the sound of wood breaking. After the tornado had passed, everything was a mess. Some of our walls were gone. The trees in our yard were bare. The storm had ripped the bark right off of them.

was it?

Mapping Weathe

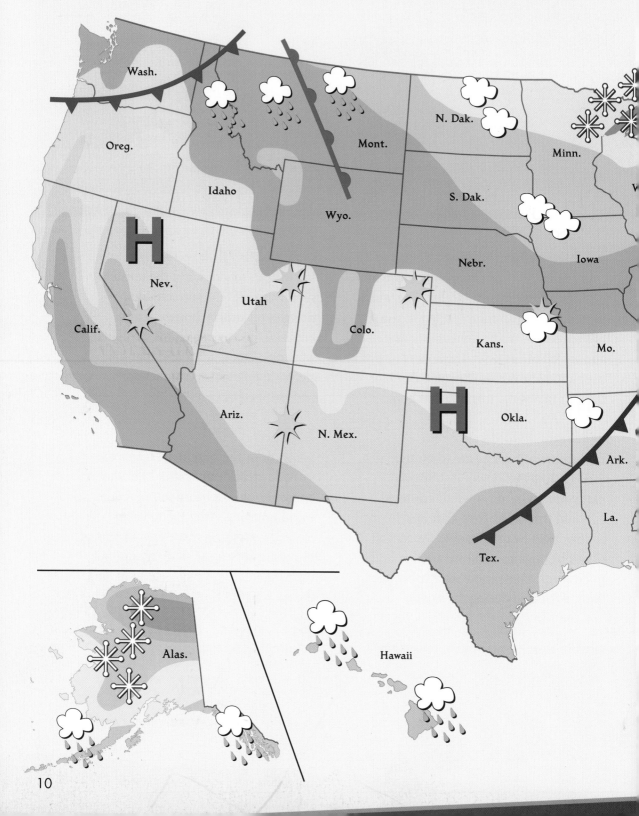

Weather maps use special symbols to show different conditions. The key tells what each symbol means. Use the key to tell what kind of weather the map shows for your state. Then pick another state. What is the weather like there?

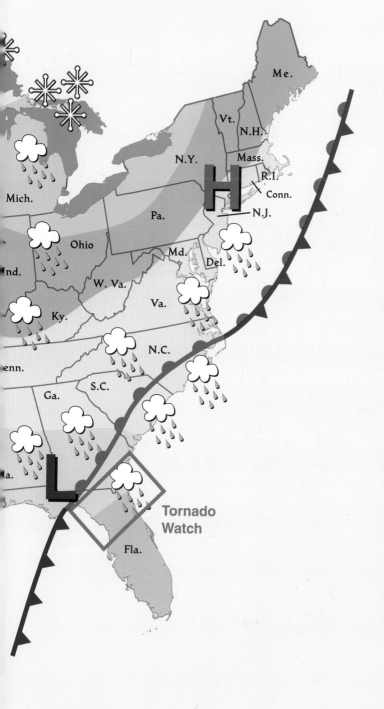

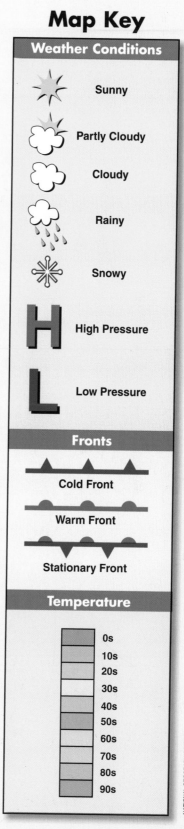

Map Key

Weather Conditions

	Sunny
	Partly Cloudy
	Cloudy
	Rainy
	Snowy
H	High Pressure
L	Low Pressure

Fronts

Cold Front

Warm Front

Stationary Front

Temperature

	0s
	10s
	20s
	30s
	40s
	50s
	60s
	70s
	80s
	90s

Tornado Watch

NATIONAL GEOGRAPHIC MAPS

Tornadoes

Twist your brain around these questions to see what you've learned about tornadoes.

1 Why do tornado chasers drive into storms?

2 Why are meteorologists interested in tornadoes?

3 How does Doppler radar help people study tornadoes?

4 Why do so many tornadoes form in Tornado Alley?

5 What does the rating scale tell about a tornado?